A Rational Counseling Primer

by Howard S. Young

Illustrated by Kenneth Aptekar

Institute for Rational-Emotive Therapy, New York, N.Y.

A Rational Counseling Primer

Published by the Institute for Rational-Emotive Therapy
45 East 65th Street, New York, N.Y. 10021

PRINTED IN THE UNITED STATES OF AMERICA

Tenth printing

ISBN-0-917476-01-8

A Rational Counseling Primer

by Howard S. Young

Illustrated by Kenneth Aptekar

People come to counseling because they are disturbed or upset with themselves, others, or the world about them.

This upsettedness might be expressed in many different ways. Some people get depressed, some worry all the time, some feel inferior or worthless, some use drugs, some develop ulcers, and some even have nervous breakdowns or commit suicide.

What causes all this suffering?

Is it the way a person was raised by his parents? A dehumanized society? An insensitive government? A rejecting boyfriend? A jealous wife? An alcoholic husband?

Maybe it's the high meat prices or an obnoxious neighbor? Or in-laws or out-laws? The untimely death of a close friend or relative? Perhaps it might have something to do with failing an important task or losing a job?

Many of us have experienced some of these events, but do they really upset or disturb us? It may seem surprising, but no outside event or circumstance can emotionally distress or make a person feel badly.

What causes us to become upset?

"YOU'RE FIRED!"
REPORT CARD
F
INCOME TAX
Amount Due—
$9,000,000
SPECIAL TODAY!
$50.00
MOTHER

It is our point of view!

This is one important basic goal of rational counseling. Showing you that it is your opinion or idea about something, not the something itself that is upsetting.

Let's go over that point again.

There is no way another person, situation, or event can make you feel angry, anxious, depressed, guilty, worthless, or inferior. You upset yourself. You are responsible for creating your own emotional reactions, especially your distressing and upsetting feelings.

People, therefore, are not disturbed by things, but by views which they take of things.

It might be helpful to look at some examples of how our thinking determines our feelings and actions.

Suppose two young children are playing in the ocean, and a big wave knocks them both down. One child might run to his mother crying and be quite frightened. The other child may be quite thrilled and decide to stay in the water until the next wave comes along. The facts, as you can see, are the same. The wave hit both children; however, it was their **evaluation** that was different. Thus, it was not the **wave** that caused the different reactions, but rather the different attitudes of the children **about** the wave.

Another example:

Read the following words:

Tree **book** **run** **sex**

Did any of the words create an emotional reaction of any kind in you? I'm willing to bet "sex" did. But, did it really, was it really the word itself?

No, it could not have been the word, for words, in and of themselves, can not cause you to feel in a certain way. The only thing that can create an emotional reaction is your **attitude** about a word.

REE
BOOK
RUN
SEX

Let's look at a somewhat more complex example.

Suppose you are on a crowded elevator and someone behind you starts poking you with an object. Being unable to turn around and protest, let's assume that like most people, you begin to get angry and upset. As the elevator lets you off on your floor you decide to give this person a piece of your mind. Just as you are about to begin, you suddenly realize the person is blind, and quite unknowingly poking you with his cane.

What happens to your anger? To your proposed tongue-lashing? Well, it's difficult to speak for everyone, but probably many people would get much less upset. They might even replace their hostile feelings with pity, and some might even feel guilty and upset with themselves for almost criticizing a handicapped person.

What caused the drastic change in feelings in the example? Very simply, new ideas or attitudes resulting from looking at the situation differently. In other words, **a change in mind caused a change in feelings.**

THE THEORY OF RATIONAL COUNSELING

The principles governing Rational Counseling are not new. They were first introduced as a way of understanding human behavior by the Greek philosophers over two thousand years ago. It was not until about twenty years ago, however, that a creative and innovative psychologist, Albert Ellis, began to use these principles in counseling and psychotherapy.

Just what are these principles?

Perhaps the most important is that **human beings have the unique capacity and ability to think and reason.** That is, no matter what kind of situations come to our attention we have an opinion, judgment, or evaluation. We may not always come up with the correct or most accurate opinion, but nevertheless we are always thinking and concluding something about our life experiences.

If we were to observe closely we would realize that we do our thinking in simple sentences and phrases. Put more simply, when we think we talk to ourselves. Although occasionally we do so out loud, for the most part, we talk to ourselves silently in our own heads.

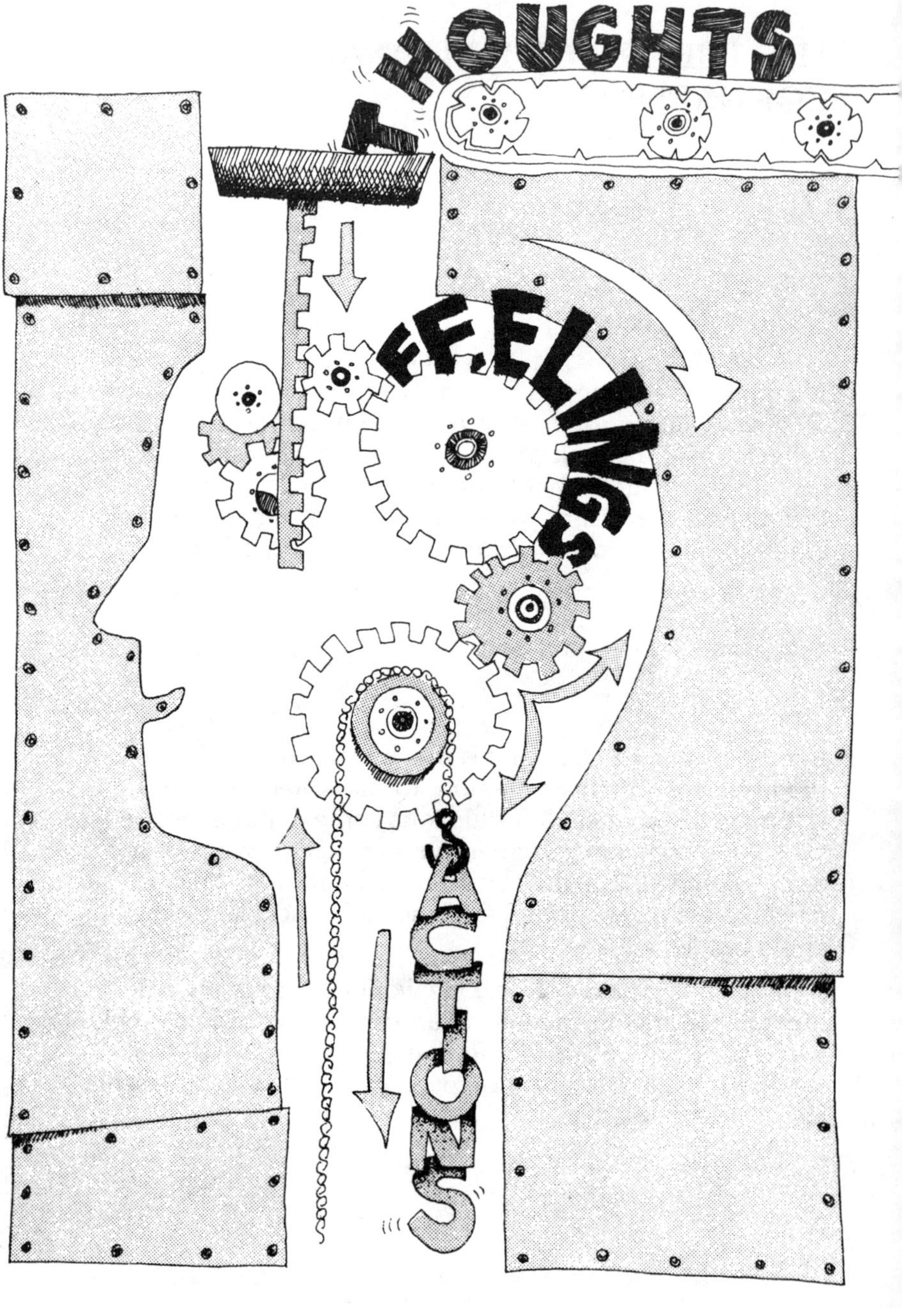
THOUGHTS
FEELINGS
ACTIONS

Often we do not realize what we tell ourselves, as much of our mental figuring goes on outside our immediate awareness. Sometimes we evaluate a situation so quickly it does not seem we thought about it at all. A prejudice is a good example of such an instantaneous or unconscious thought process.

Emotions (leaving out those caused by physical contact, drugs, or hormones) depend on our point of view. **We feel the way we think.** The more extreme our point of view about an event, the more intensely we will feel about the same event.

Our actions usually, although not necessarily always, follow our feelings. What we do will often depend upon how we evaluated and felt about a particular situation.

Thinking, therefore, produces feelings which in turn generate actions.

When our thoughts and ideas are based on superstitions, prejudices, folklore, or other false assumptions, then the feelings and actions that follow will often cause problems and difficulties.

When such fictitious thinking is well learned and long practiced it easily becomes a habit. The emotions and behavior that result from such chronically unrealistic thinking are usually called **neurotic** or **disturbed.**

Thus, when we say someone is "*emotionally disturbed*" what we mean is that his evaluation of a particular situation is incorrect, and that, as a result, he suffers upsetting feelings and behaves in unproductive or unsatisfying ways.

The objective of Rational Counseling is to teach people to recognize inaccuracies in their thinking and arrive at a more realistic view of themselves and their surroundings.

THE A-B-C OF EMOTIONS

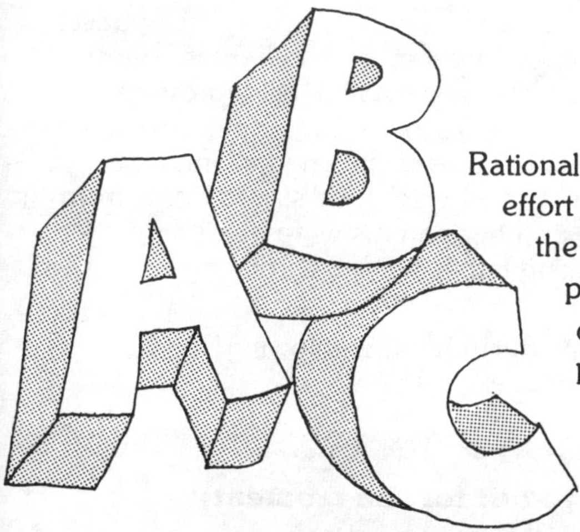

Rational Counseling makes every effort to be uncomplicated and to the point. This *"simplicity"* principle is followed closely in understanding people and helping them solve their problems.

How? By following the simple A-B-C format. It goes like this:

Something happens, like you get criticized, and **you react, like you get angry or defensive.**

The point here is that getting criticized **does not cause** the anger or the defensiveness. Holding to our premise that it is one's attitude or belief that causes us to become upset we have the following:

A. **Something happens (criticism)**

B. **Attitude or belief (about the criticism)**

C. **Reaction as a result of the belief (anger or defensiveness**

AN EXAMPLE OF A-B-C

Here is a real life example of the A-B-C principle:

Recently, a 16 year old girl came in to see me very much upset because her steady boyfriend left her for another girl. She described her feelings, which were evident, as depression, anger (at her boyfriend), worthlessness, and hopelessness. As a result of these feelings she claimed she cried all the time, could not eat, threatened to kill herself, and stayed home from school. In addition, she and her parents were quarreling over the least little thing, making family life quite irritating.

In the A-B-C format she concluded the following:

A. **(Event)**
I got rejected.)

B. **(we will leave out for the moment)**

C. **(Emotional reaction)**
I got depressed, angry, felt I was no good

and

I cried, could not eat, threatened to kill myself, stayed home from school and quarreled with my parents.

Since I am a rational counselor, I realized that **A** did not cause C. I further realized that a rejection may have practical disadvantages, but it need not be considered a catastrophe. Only one's point of view can do that. Therefore, I asked her what her thoughts and opinions about this situation were. Although at first she claimed she did not have any opinions, after a little while she came up with the following:

"It's not fair that he did such a mean thing. I can't stand being treated this way. He has no right. He shouldn't have done it. I'd like to get even, like go back with him and then drop him. I can't think much of myself now, who would ever want a reject, I feel completely worthless."

With this new information, it became easy to see why this young lady was so upset, and now we can probably fill in the **B** part of our format:

A. **(Event)**
I got rejected

B. **(Beliefs or thoughts)**
I can't stand it.
He has no right.
It shouldn't be.
I'd like to get even.
I'm a reject.
I'm worthless.

C. **(Emotional reaction)**
I got depressed, angry, felt I was no good

and

I cried, could not eat, threatened to kill myself stayed home from school and quarreled with my parents.

The above beliefs are an excellent example of **irrational thinking** and would lead anyone of similar convictions to be most unhappy and upset.

However, if you are like many people, including the girl in the example, you may at first have difficulty accepting that these ideas are irrational and based on opinion rather than fact. It is quite possible that many people would readily agree that these ideas are rational under the circumstances; that there is no other way of looking at the situation; and that anyone would have thought and felt the same way.

Since this would not be an unusual response, it is important that we now examine closely what irrational thinking is, and how it is caused.

SOME IRRATIONAL IDEAS THAT LEAD TO EMOTIONAL UPSET

What kind of ideas cause people to get upset? Are there some standard ideas that lead to unhappiness?

There certainly are—a good number. However, almost all misery producing ideas have one characteristic in common. They contain either one or two words!

AWFUL and **SHOULD.**

AWFUL includes a host of attitudinal exaggerations and extremes such as **terrible, horrible,** or **dreadful.** Awfulizing is often expressed when we say to ourselves and others:

It's dreadful!
Oh, my God!
I can't stand it!

SHOULD includes such attitudinal absolutes as **must, ought, got, need,** and **insist.** Should is expressed when we say:

It shouldn't be!
I have to be loved!
I've got to be first!

Of course, it is not the words or expressions themselves but the attitude or general meaning behind the words or expressions that cause the problems.

RRIBL
AWFUL

The attitude behind **AWFUL** is almost always an unrealistic exaggeration. When you awfulize you translate disappointments into disasters. It is like saying that 2 plus 2 equals 400 or that someone *over* drowned. Such thinking usually makes an unfortunate situation worse when it need only be considered unfortunate.

The attitude behind **SHOULD** is almost always an unrealistic demand. When you tell yourself a **should** you translate desires into demands. It is like saying red should be blue or that it shouldn't be raining when it is. **"Should"** means I absolutely must have things my way, and I must not be inconvenienced when I do not want to be.

What do you do with your awful's and should's?

You vigorously and stubbornly challenge and question their validity.

How?

Very simply, by always asking the question, *WHY?*

You question your **awfuls** by asking, ***why** is it awful— where is my proof?*

If you examine any situation closely, you will discover that **nothing is awful.** You might discover that a particular situation is unfortunate or even highly unpleasant and that there may be some realistic disadvantages involved. But it is unlikely that anything is truly terrible or horrible.

Looking at things in this manner when you face a frustrating event you might very well be emotional, perhaps highly so, but not hysterical or panic-stricken. You don't have to *flip out* or get bent out of shape when things become difficult. Granted, inconvenience and disadvantage clearly exist in the world. But awfulness and terribleness are exaggerations; they are monsters and demons you make up in your own head.

You question **shoulds** by asking *why should it be—who said so?* The answer to a **should** is, *It doesn't **have** to be.* Nothing has to be the way you want, and although it might be better if things were the way you want—that doesn't mean they **must, ought,** or **should** be that way.

It is important to realize that **reality is reality, not what you want it to be.** You are not owed certain desirable satisfactions (such as love, approval, success or prestige) even if you experienced a deprived childhood, suffered many hardships, or someone is doing better than you. YOU DO NOT RUN THE UNIVERSE. THINGS DO NOT HAVE TO GO YOUR WAY!

AN EXAMPLE OF A-B-C-D-E

We will use an example to illustrate how you can begin to challenge your irrational beliefs.

Let's take the case of a 24 year old mechanic who was always putting himself down for making mistakes and claimed he suffered from an *inferiority complex.* Most recently he forgot to complete an oil change which brought some criticism from both his annoyed customer and his unhappy boss. In a subsequent counseling session he described himself as feeling inferior or worthless.

A. **(Event)**
Making a mistake—forgetting the oil change.

B. **(Belief or thought)**
(Not yet known)

C. **(Emotional reaction)**
Hurt feelings—worthlessness, inferiority.

Now what about the **B** beliefs?

Here is what the young mechanic reported was going through his mind:

Oh my God, I forgot the oil change. Not another goof-up. I shouldn't have been so stupid. I should have remembered such an easy thing. How could I just forget. What a jerk I am. How could I be such an idiot.

Did you notice all the **awfuls** and **shoulds**? Did you notice that they lead to self-downing, and self-blaming. In other words, **awfuls** and **shoulds,** regardless of how expressed, can cause you to dislike and put yourself down.

Let's slightly edit our **B**'s and put them in where they belong.

A. **(Event)**
Making a mistake—forgetting the oil change.

B. **(Beliefs or thoughts)**
It's awful I made the mistake.
I shouldn't have made it.
Now that I made such an error I am a total idiot.

C. **(Emotional reaction)**
Hurt feelings—worthlessness, inferiority.

In many ways this example is not particularly different from that of the 15 year old girl who lost her boyfriend. Both the criticized mechanic and the rejected young lady told themselves enough **awfuls** and **shoulds** to upset anyone.

what a JERK!
I'm such an IDIOT!
I SHOULD have remembered.

How do you begin to overcome such a situation?

By adding **D** and **E** to our format.
That's right, **A-B-C-D-E.**

D means to dispute, question, to challenge. Remember, the first step in handling awfuls and shoulds is to ask, *why*.

Using our above example:

D. **Why** is it awful I made the mistake?

D. **Why** shouldn't I have made the mistake?

D. **Why** does making a mistake make me stupid or a total idiot?

Now let's get to **"E"**.

E is the heart of rational counseling. It is the point at which we logically, rationally, and sensibly anwer our **whys.**

Back to our example:

D. **Why is it awful that I made the mistake?**
E. It isn't awful. It is irritating and frustrating because no one particularly likes to make mistakes, but does this make it such a big deal? Hardly! It's already a regrettable situation-so there's no use stretching it into an AWFUL situation.

D. **Why shouldn't I have made the mistake?**
E. It would be better if I did not make the mistake, but there is no evidence to prove that I absolutely **must not** make a mistake (even with an easy task). That is what my silly **should** is, an absolute demand that I be perfect—that I not do what I just did, make a mistake.

D. **Why does making a mistake make me stupid or a total idiot?**
E. It doesn't, except in my own head—and that is the problem. I believe that doing something wrong makes me an idiot, jerk, or whatever. Nothing I can do can make me anything; I am not my behavior. Just like a flat tire does not make a whole car worthless, a mistake does not make me a total idiot. Besides, as long as I live on this earth I will make mistakes, so I might as well get used to it, and stop exaggerating their importance and insisting I don't make any. Instead of blaming myself, it would be far better for me to use all that energy towards **correcting** my mistakes, if possible.

Because **D** and **E** are important final steps in overcoming emotional misery, let's once again use an illustration to further clarify this straight thinking process.

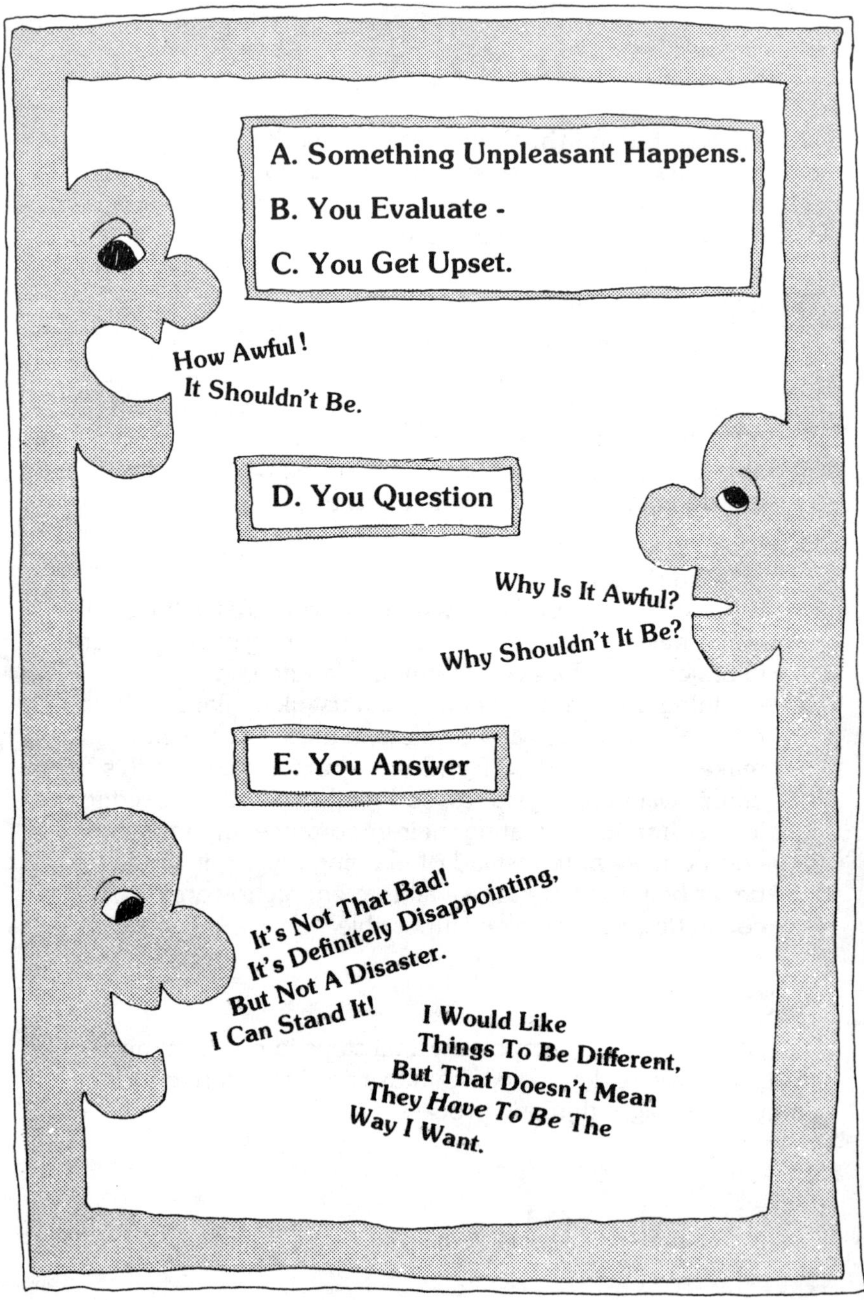
A. Something Unpleasant Happens.
B. You Evaluate -
C. You Get Upset.
How Awful!
It Shouldn't Be.
D. You Question
Why Is It Awful?
Why Shouldn't It Be?
E. You Answer
It's Not That Bad!
It's Definitely Disappointing,
But Not A Disaster.
I Can Stand It!
I Would Like
Things To Be Different,
But That Doesn't Mean
They *Have* To Be The
Way I Want.

HOW DO YOU CHANGE?

Is that all there is to it? Is it really that simple to overcome emotional difficulties?

Yes and No!

Yes, because the source of your emotional difficulties has to do with your unrealistic point of view, and challenging that point of view and correcting it is the best way to overcome emotional distress.

No, because it's not quite that easy. Just knowing is not enough, although it is an important first step. It takes conscious effort, hard work, and practice. Remember, we are talking about habits-thinking and attitudinal habits—and, as you are aware, habits are very difficult to overcome.

Irrational ideas are not given up easily, and at first it may seem that rational thinking does not work at all; that no matter how much you challenge your **awfuls** and **shoulds,** you may still stay angry, depressed, anxious and the like.

This is not an unusual initial reaction. It might be helpful to realize that you are not just working to overcome faulty thinking habits. You are also working to overcome your own natural, human tendency to think incorrectly in the first place.

Yes, humans normally have difficulty thinking straight. It is, therefore, not surprising if your first efforts at rational thinking were unsuccessful. However, stubborn human nature and long-practiced, well-learned ideas can be changed. Both will usually yield to hard work and effort.

Habits, therefore, only stay habits when they are left alone. Self-defeating ideas remain so when they are accepted without question. If you vigorously and consistently question and challenge the ideas and beliefs behind your uncomfortable feelings you will discover that, in time, you will become more and more free of negative emotions.

In other words, if you truly put in effort and **lots of practice,** after a period of time, the probability is that:

1. You will not get **as** upset.
2. You will not get upset **as often.**
3. You will not get upset **as long.**

SUMMARY

Insight #1
Upsetting feelings come from upsetting ideas.

Insight #2
You stay upset because you keep telling yourself upsetting ideas over and over again.

Insight #3
Conscious effort and hard work will overcome upsetting ideas. You do this by constantly challenging and uprooting irrational ideas and replacing them with constructive, sensible ideas.